AF260903

Dedication

This book is dedicated to my daughter who reminded me that God really does make each human so very Purrrfect!!!

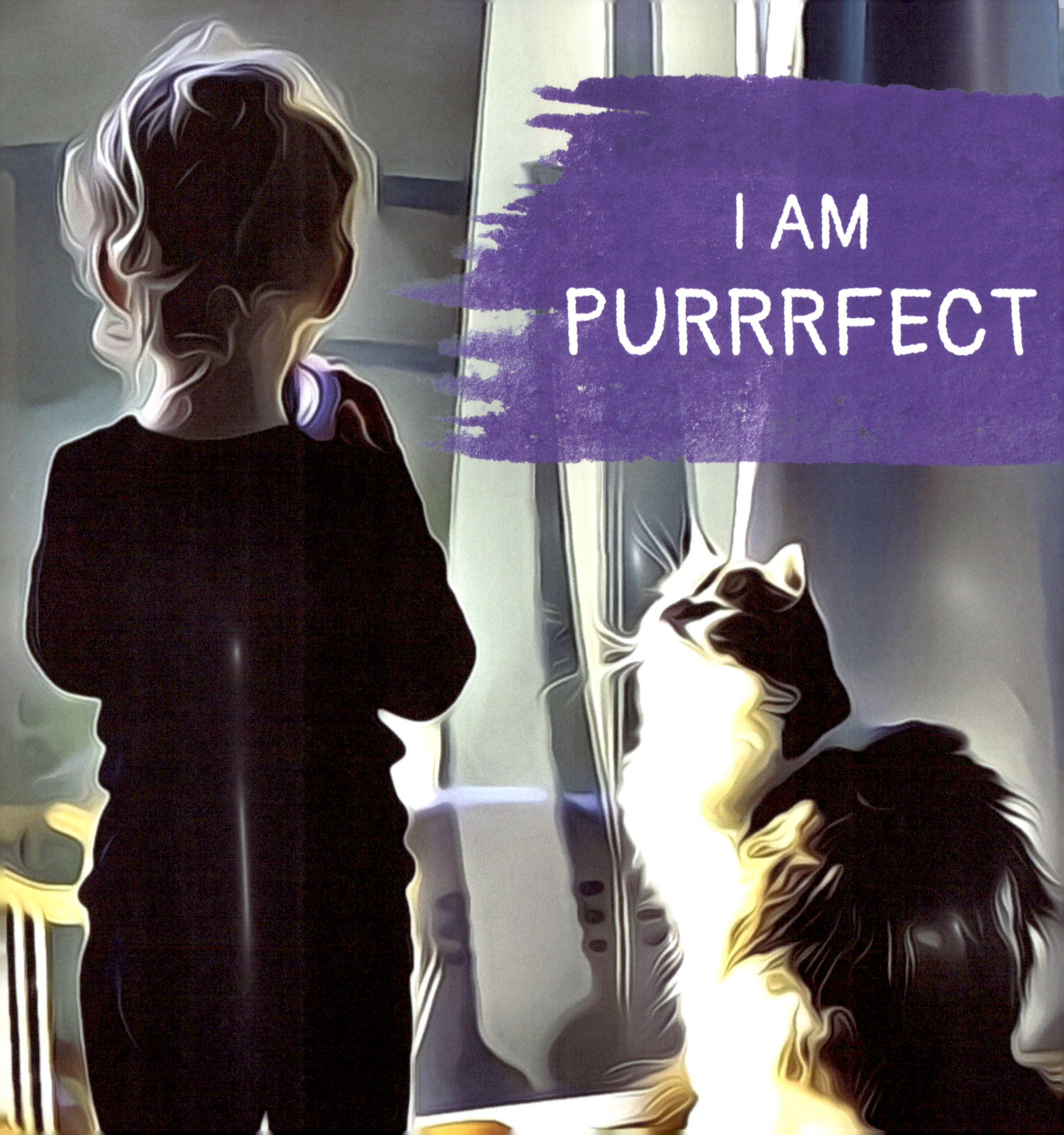
I AM
PURRRFECT

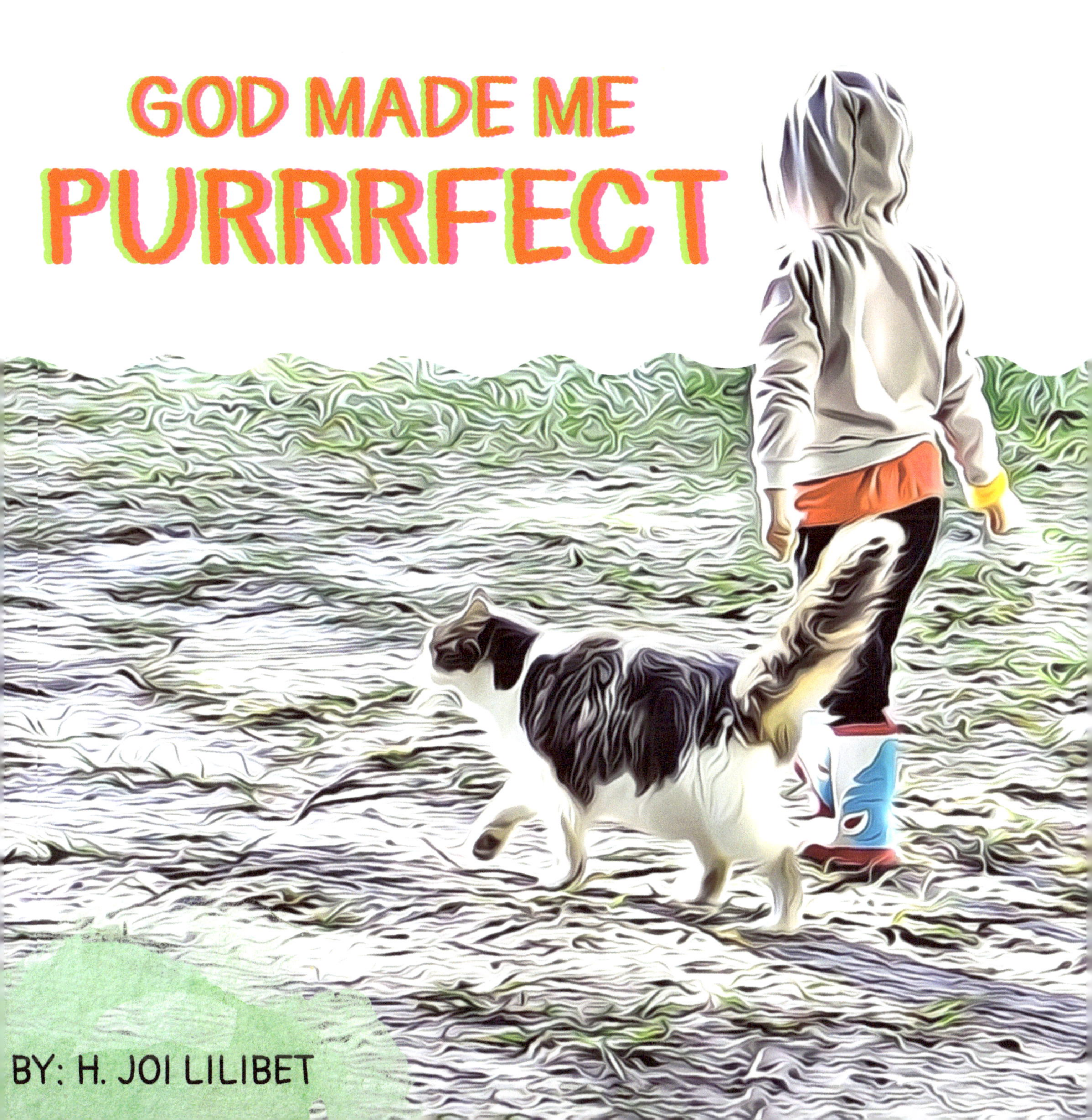

GOD MADE ME
PURRRFECT
BY: H. JOI LILIBET

GOD MADE ME PURRRFECT

Copyright © 2026 by H. JOI LILIBET
All rights reserved.

No portion of this book may be reproduced or utilized in any form or by any means — electronic or mechanical, including photocopying or recording, or by any information storage and retrieval system — without written permission from the author.

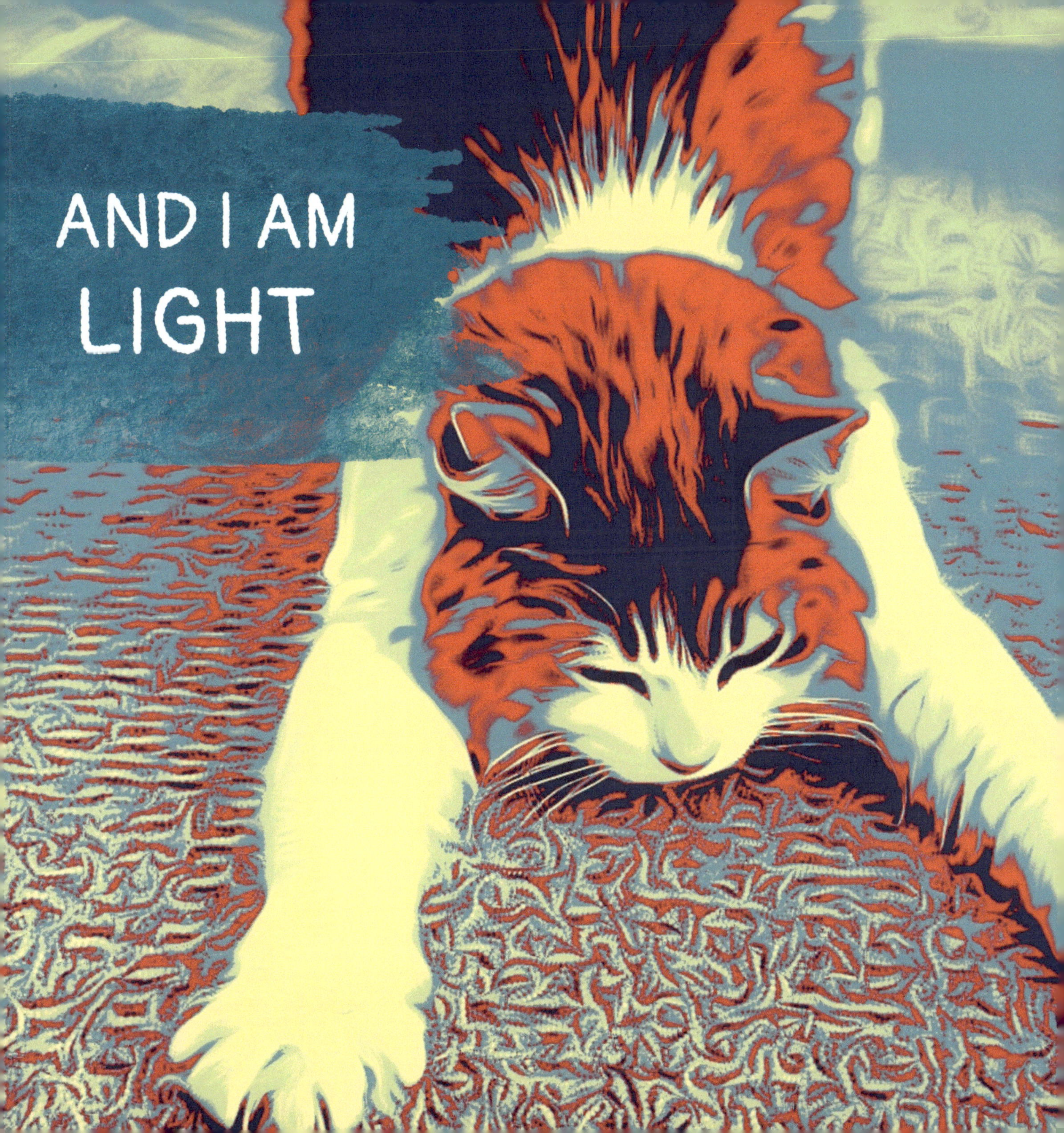
AND I AM
LIGHT

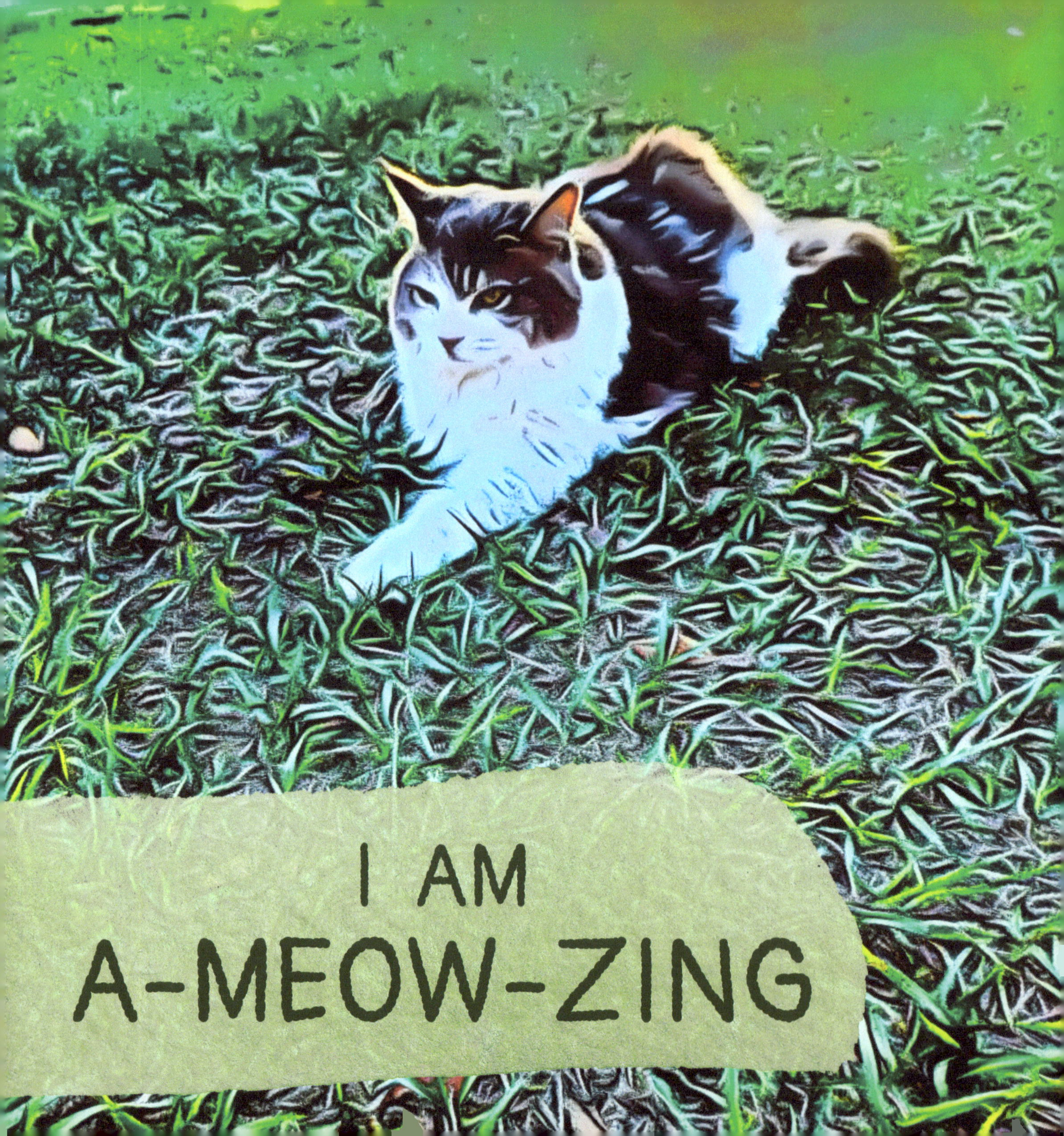
I AM
A-MEOW-ZING

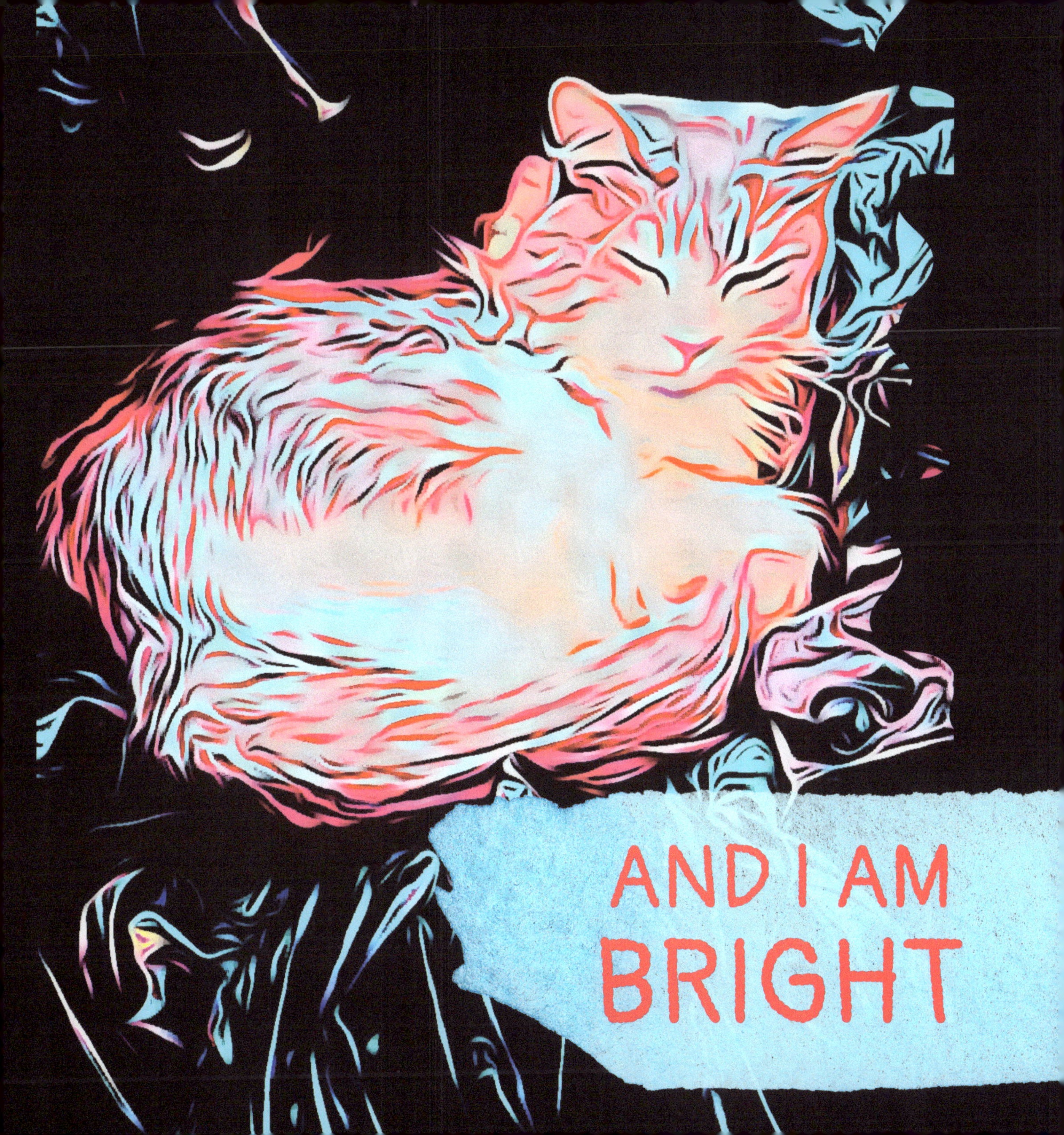

AND I AM
BRIGHT

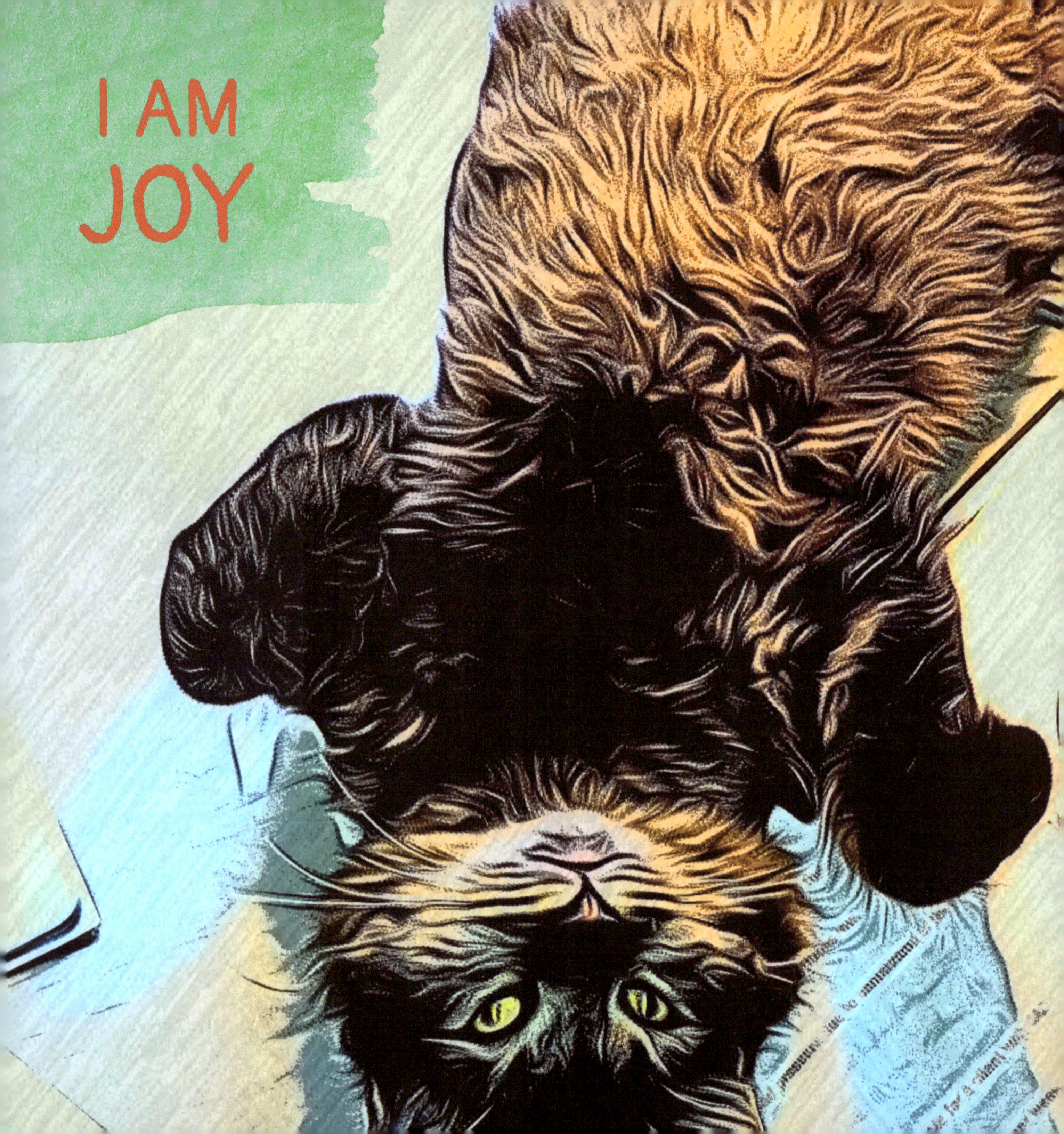
I AM
JOY

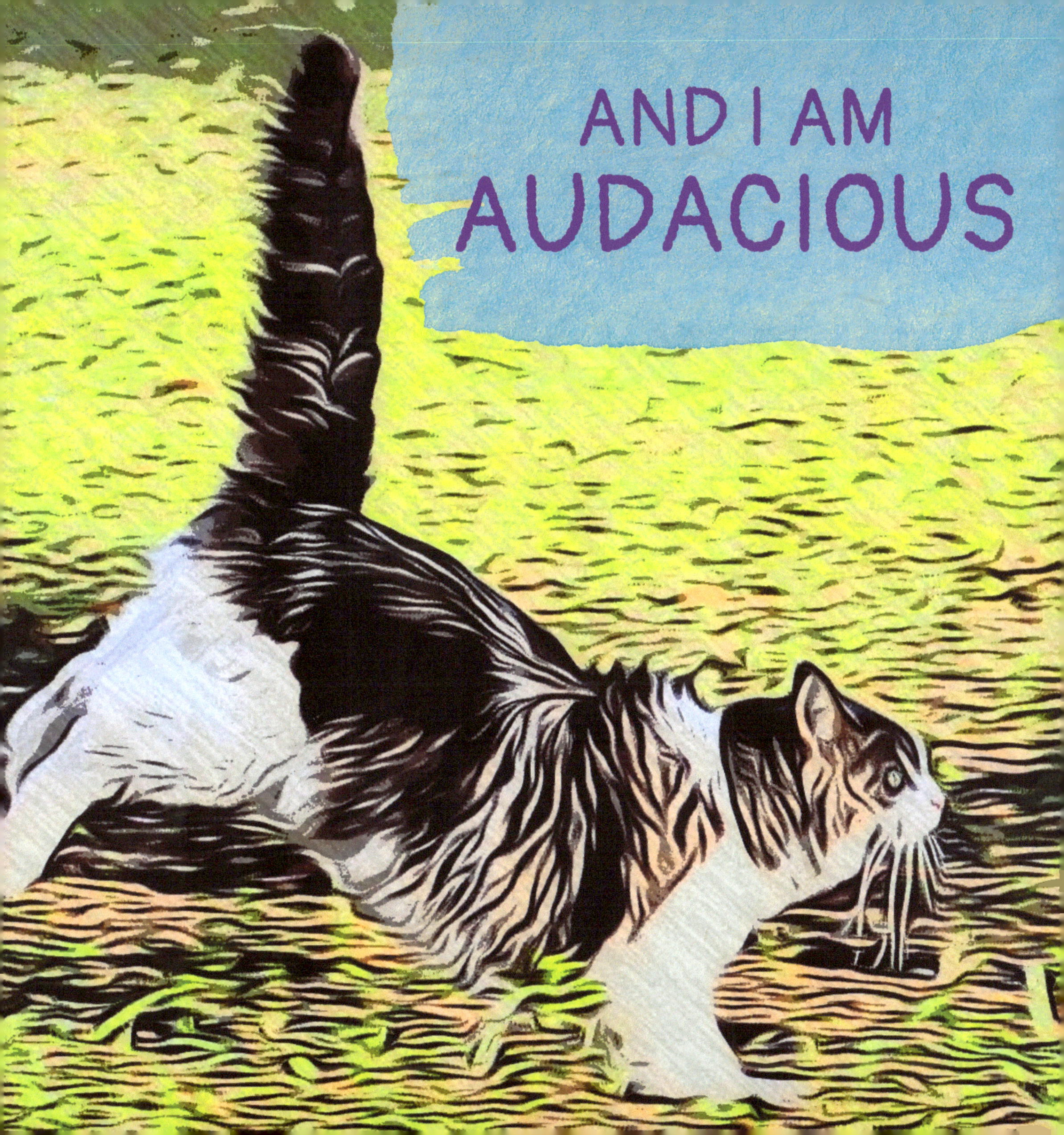

AND I AM
AUDACIOUS

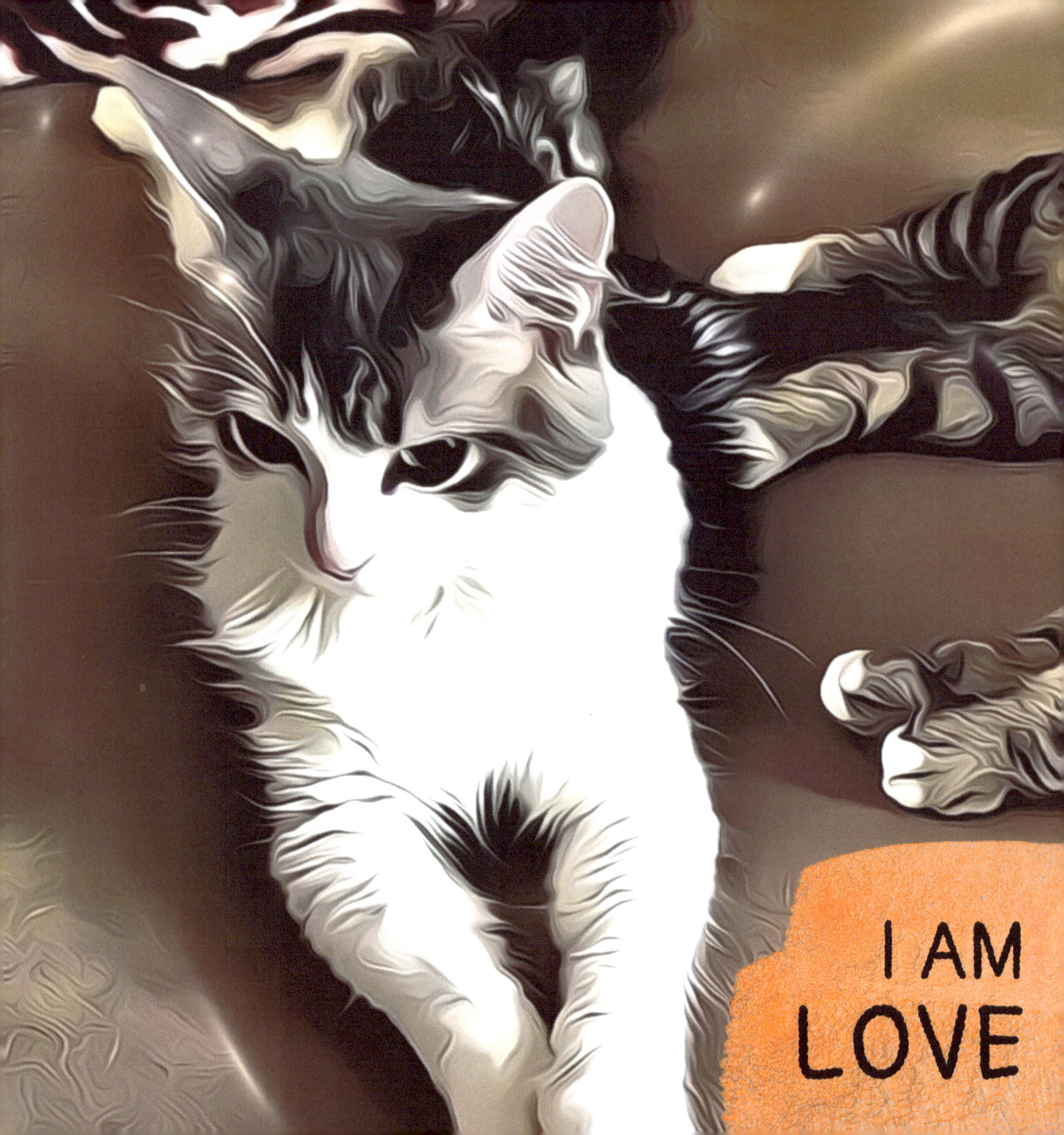
I AM
LOVE

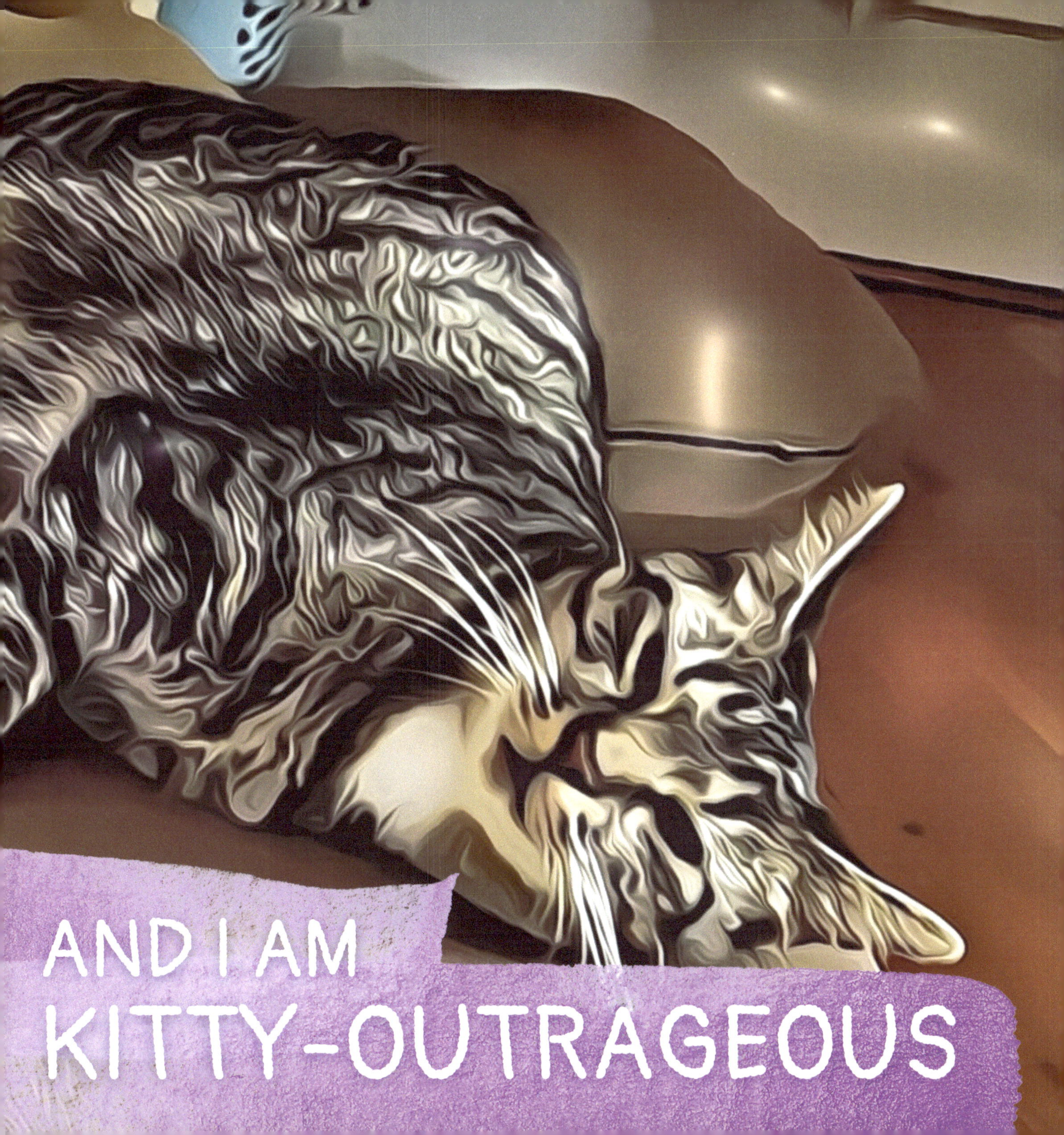

AND I AM
KITTY-OUTRAGEOUS

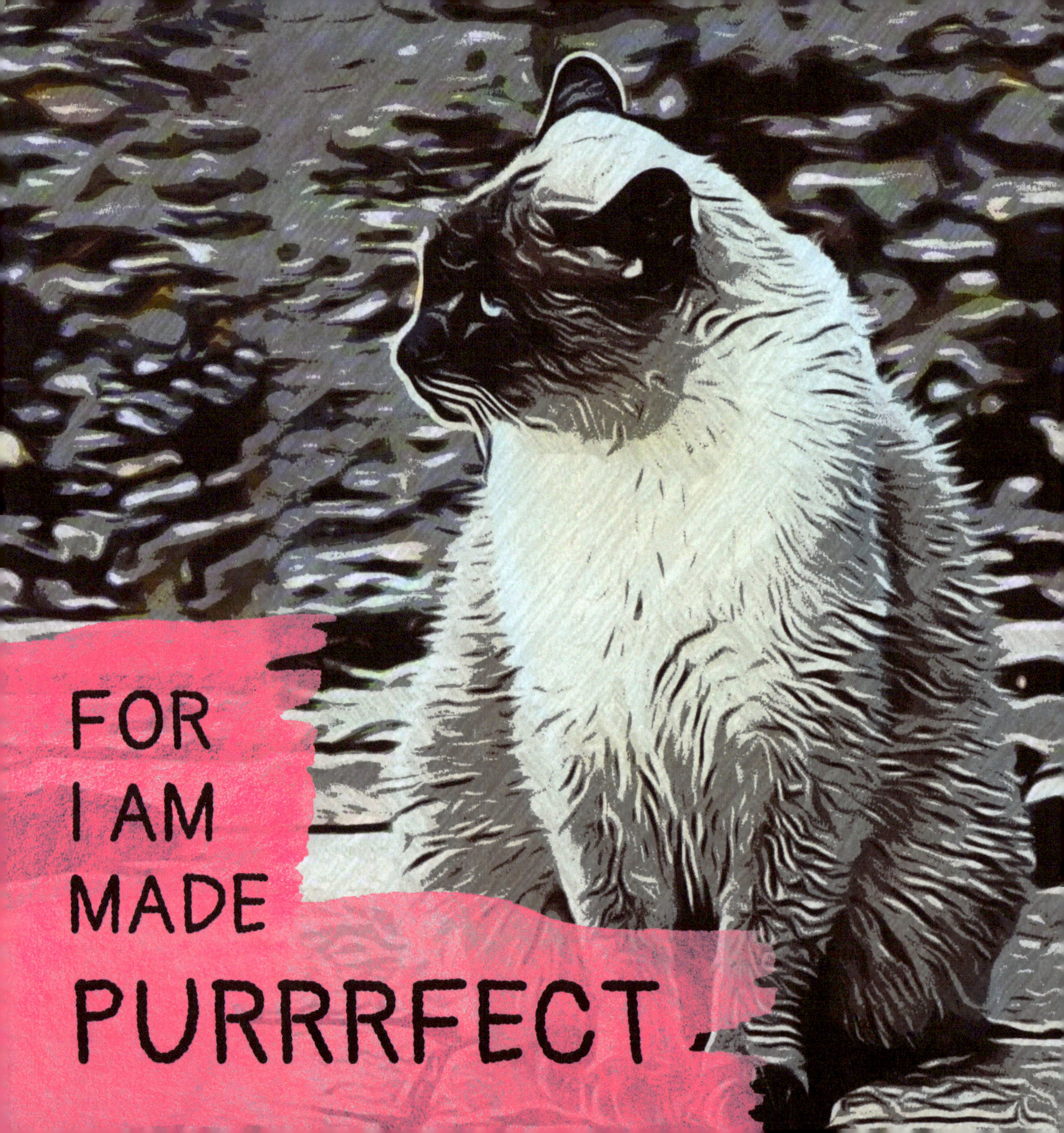

FOR
I AM
MADE
PURRRFECT

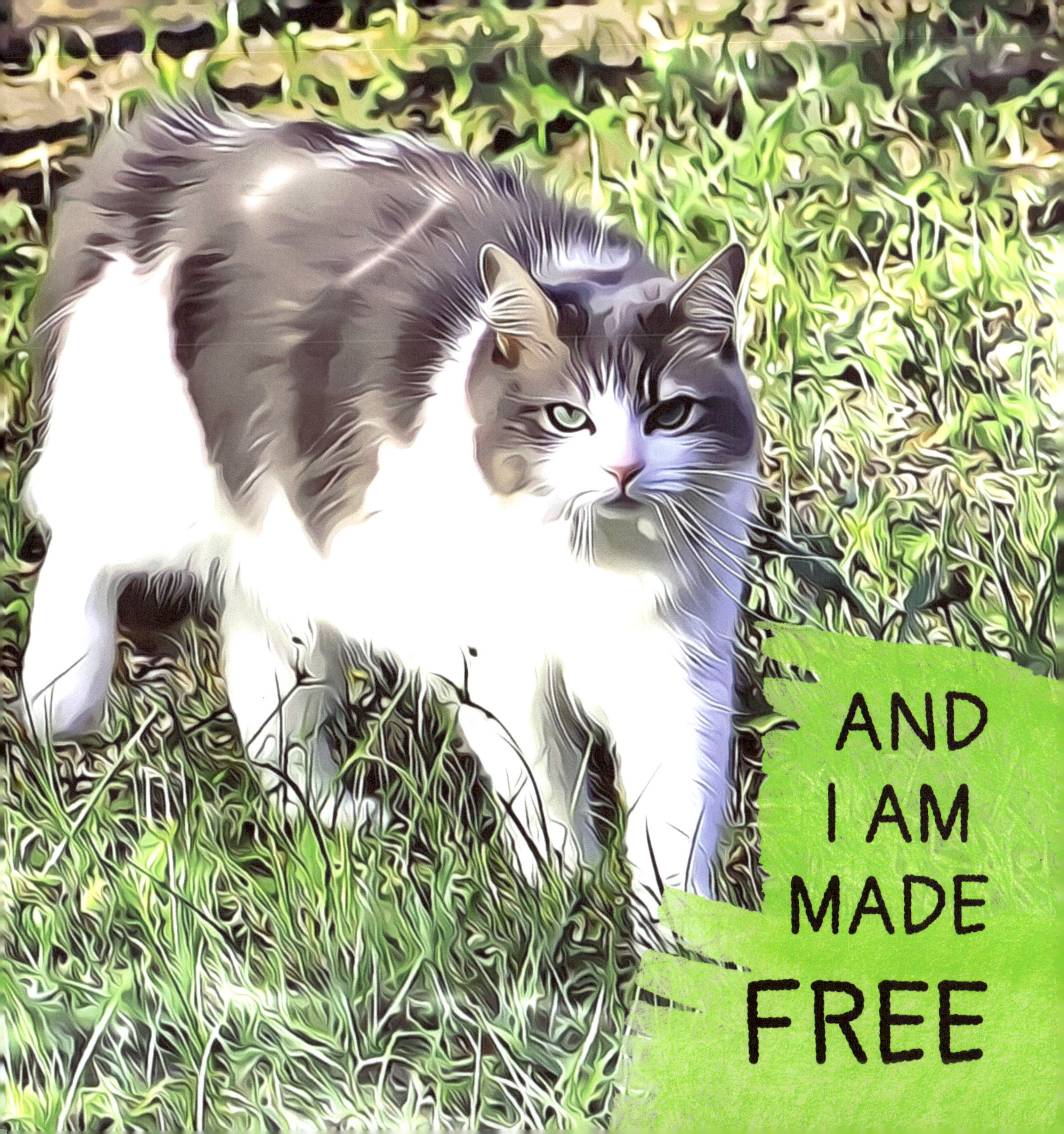

AND
I AM
MADE
FREE

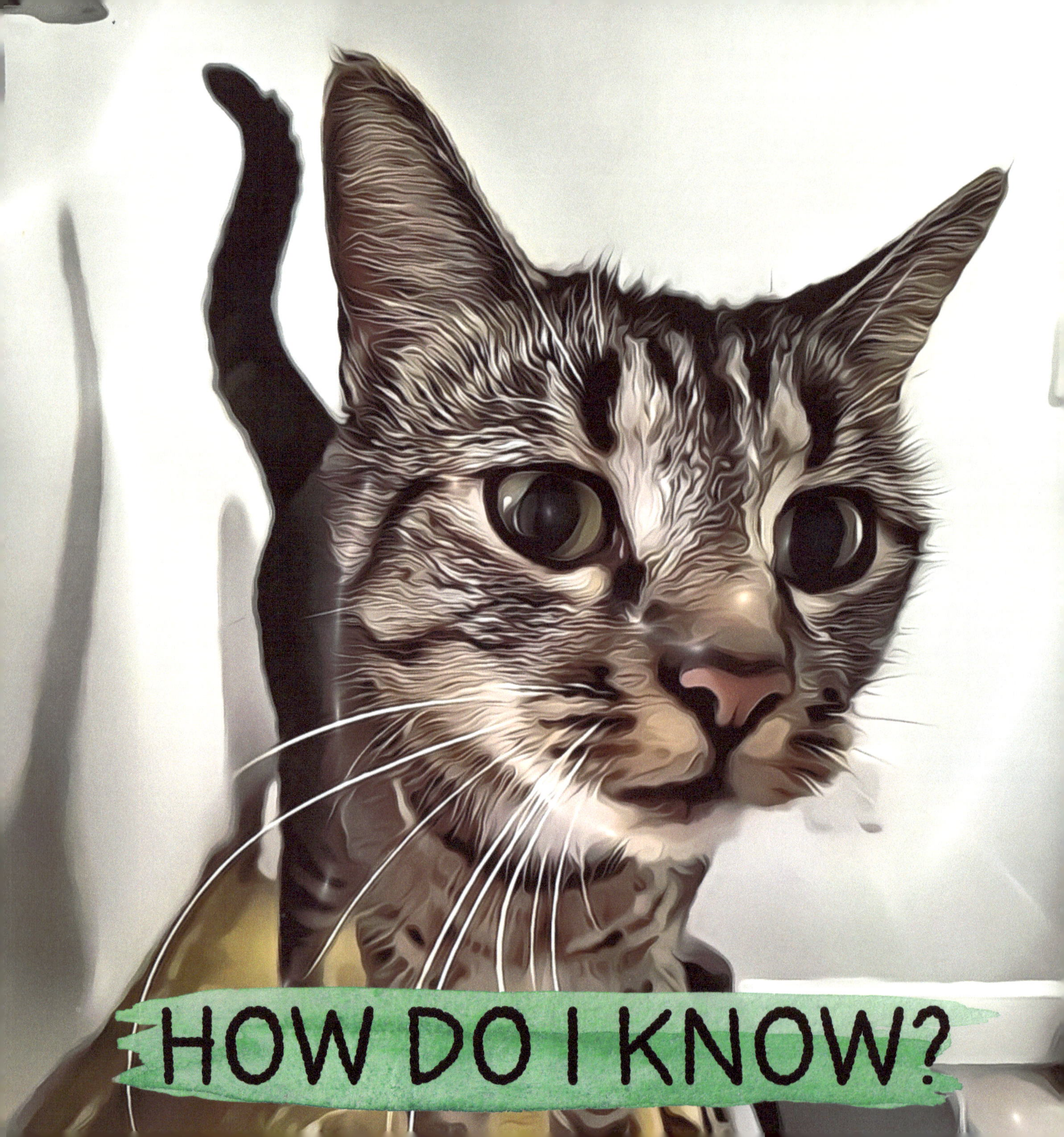
HOW DO I KNOW?

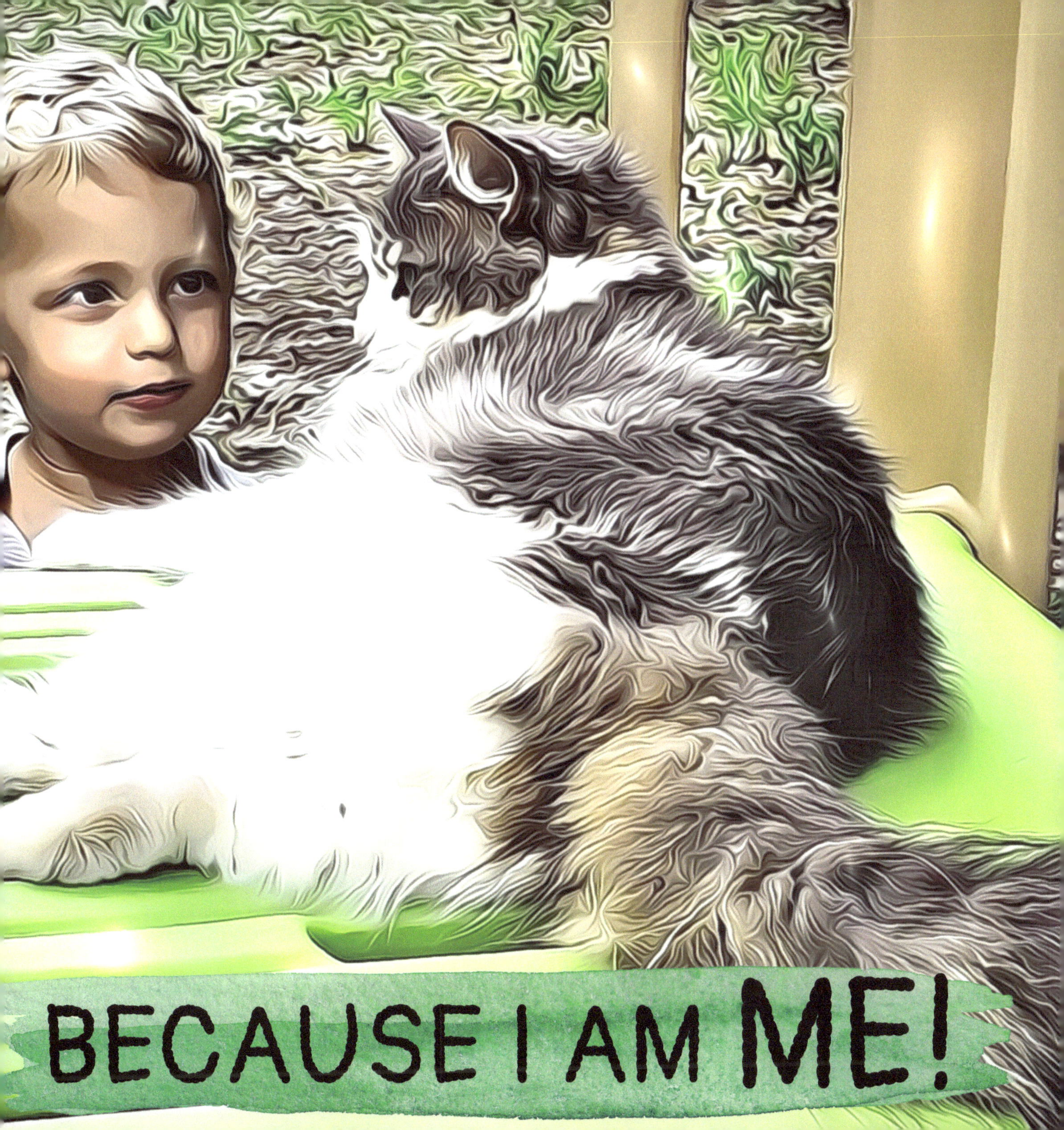
BECAUSE I AM ME!

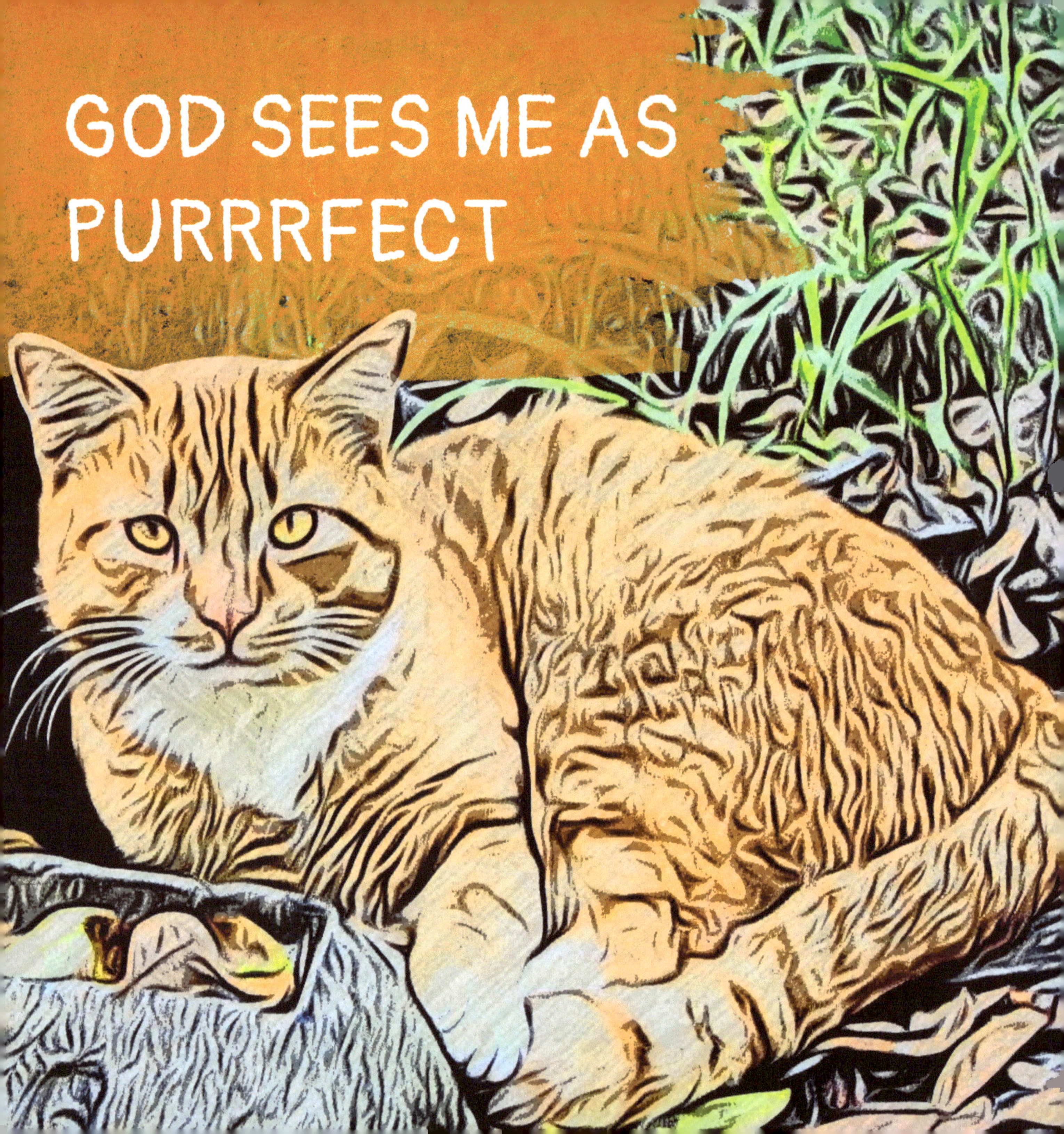
GOD SEES ME AS
PURRRFECT

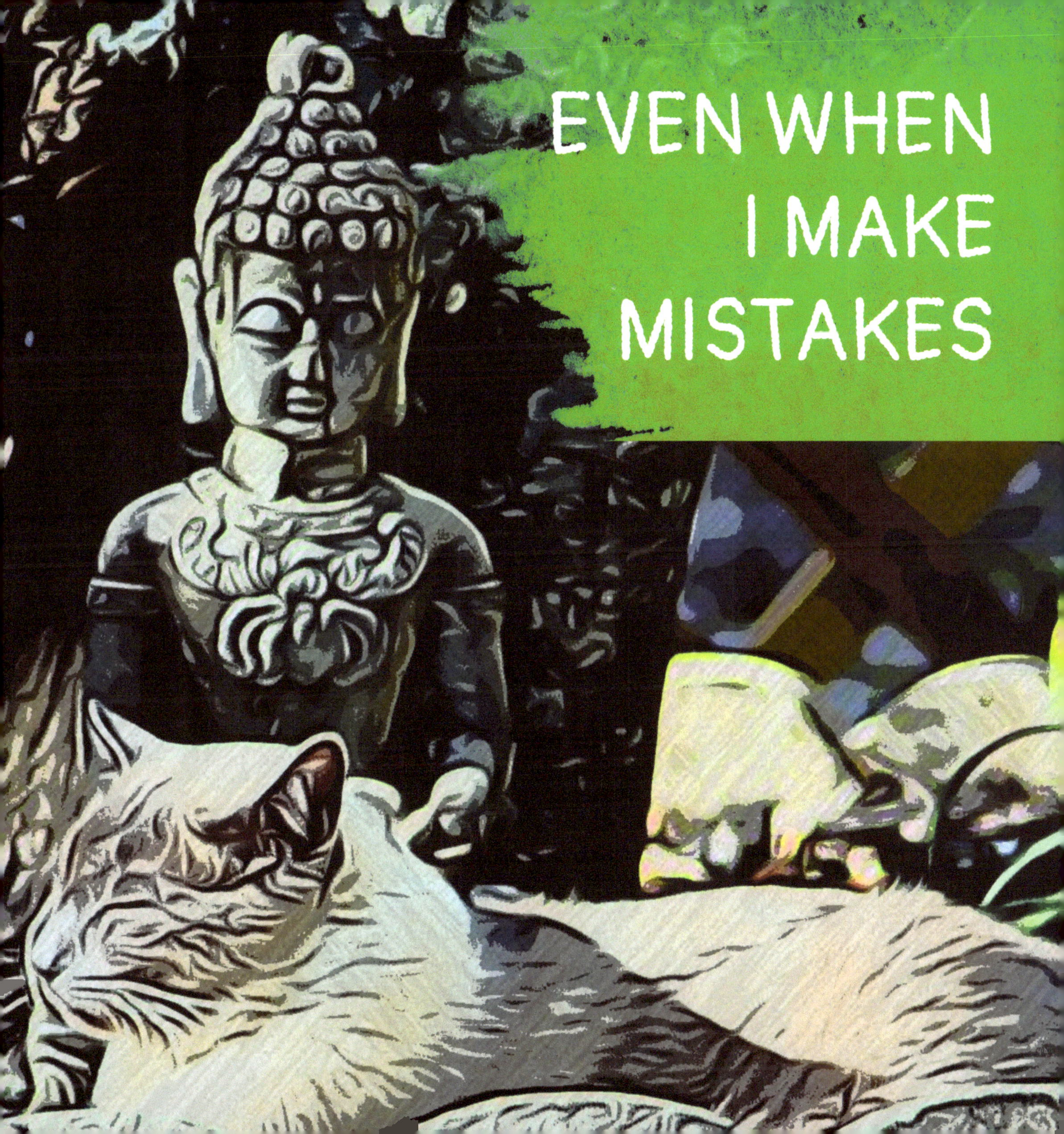
EVEN WHEN
I MAKE
MISTAKES

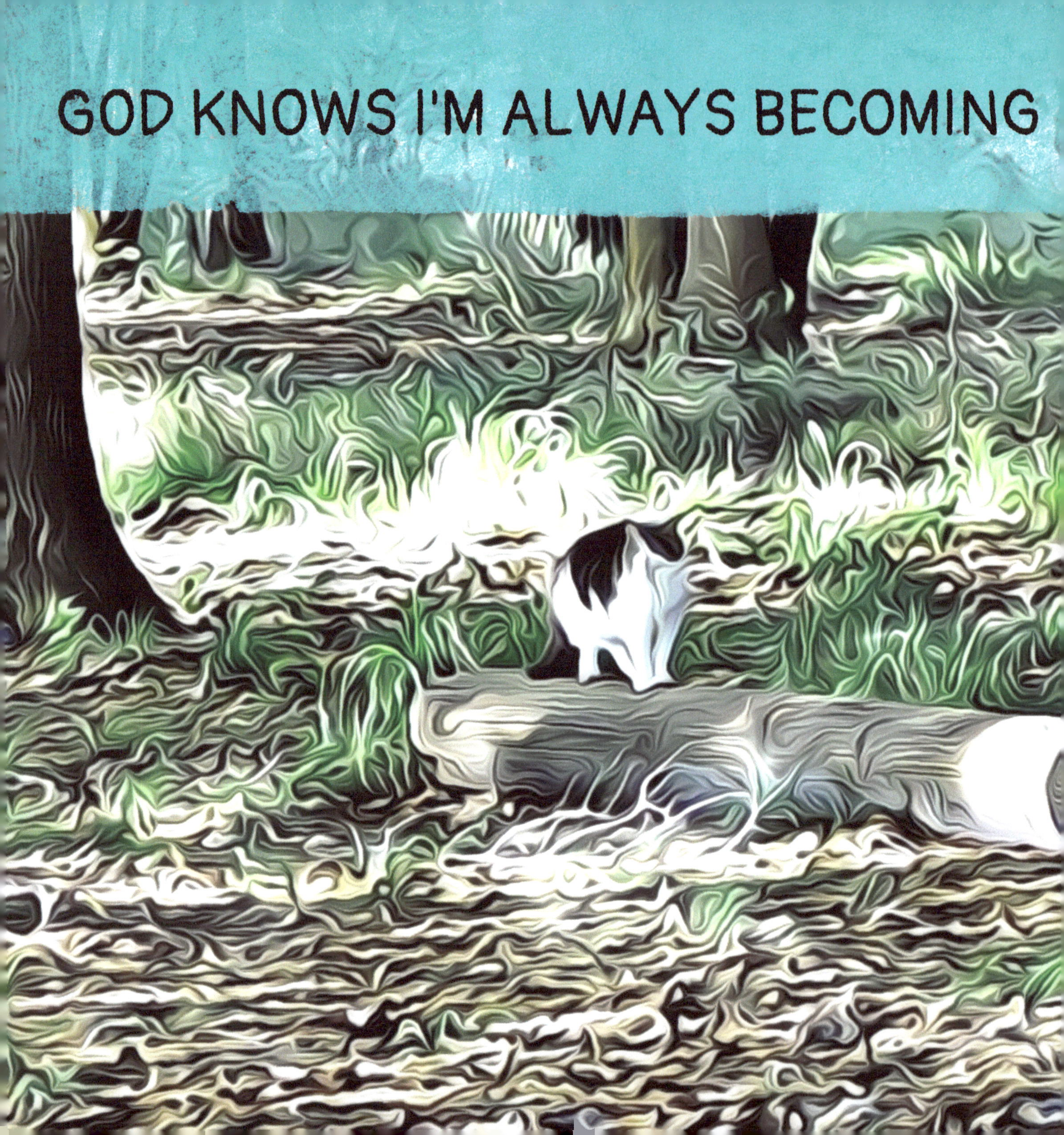

GOD KNOWS I'M ALWAYS BECOMING

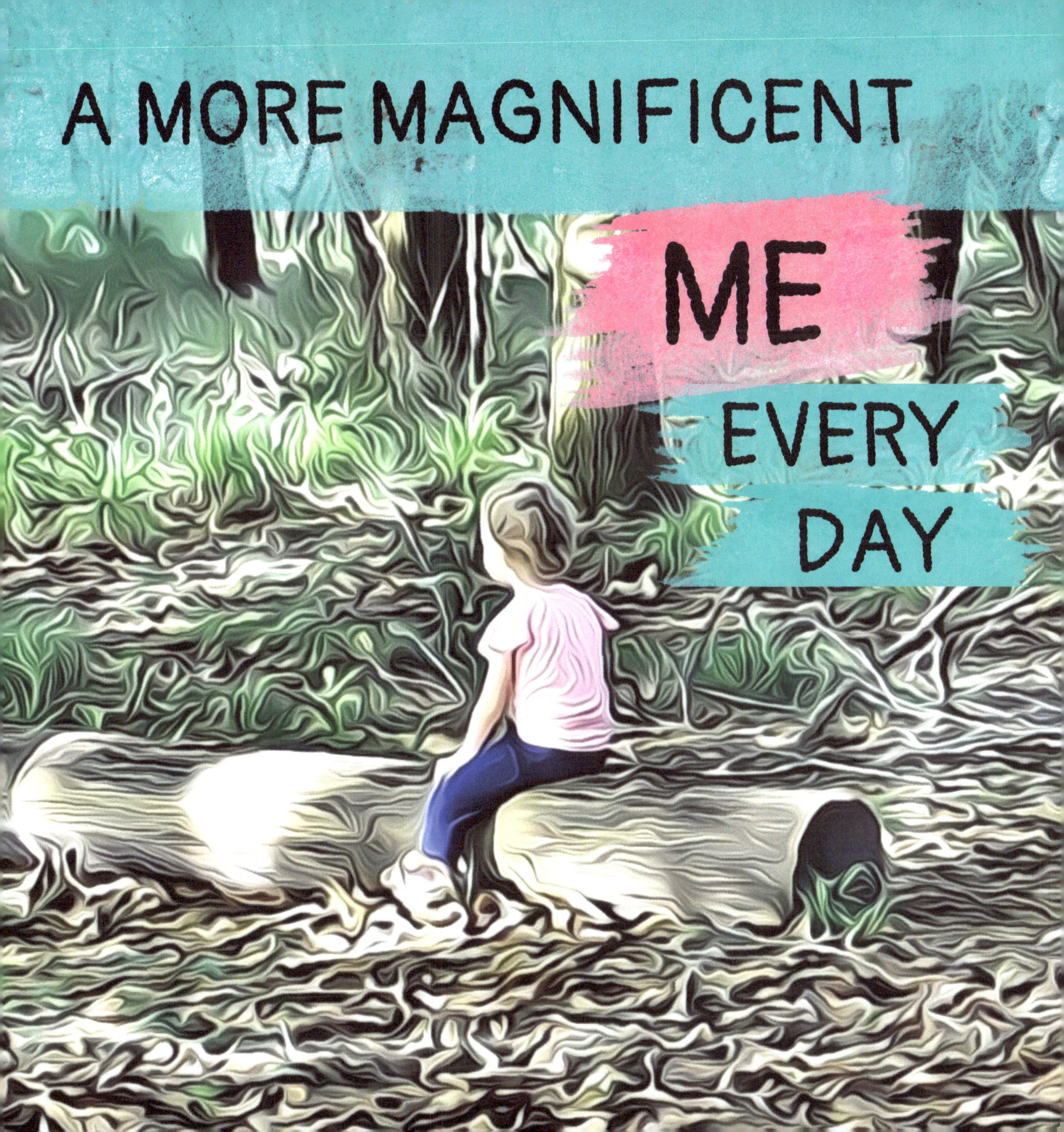

A MORE MAGNIFICENT
ME
EVERY
DAY

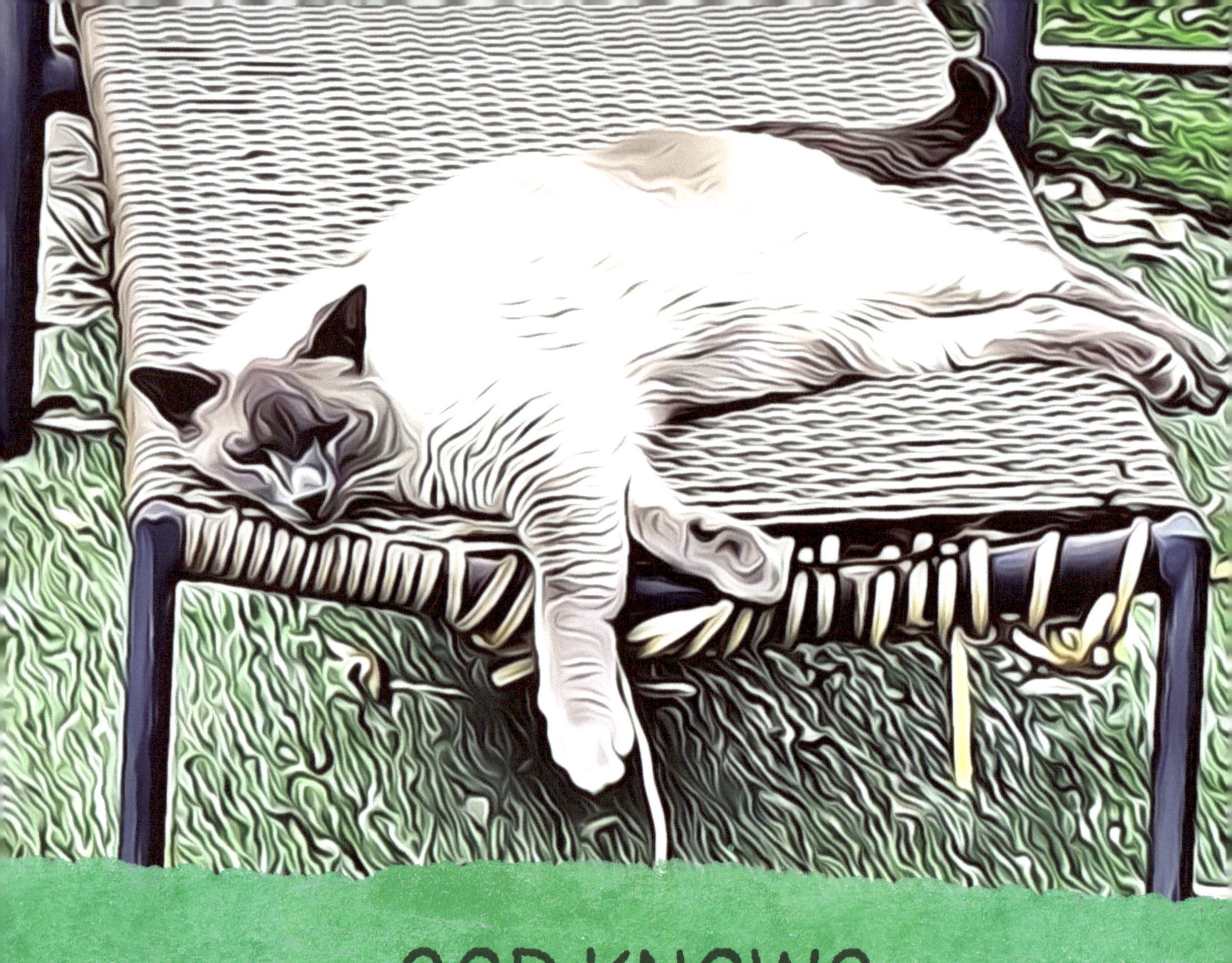

GOD KNOWS
I AM
UNDER CONSTRUCTION

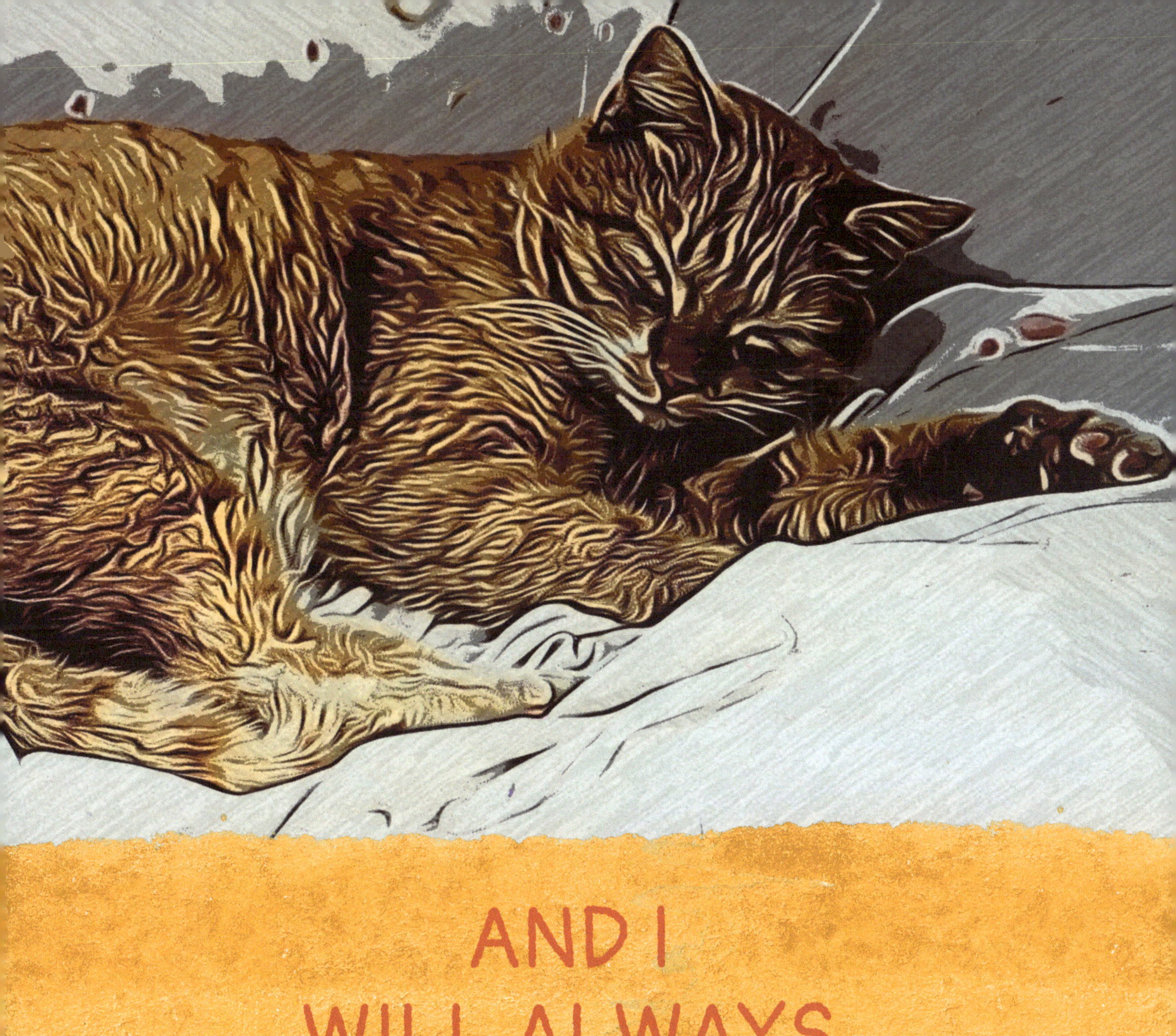

AND I
WILL ALWAYS
LEARN & GROW

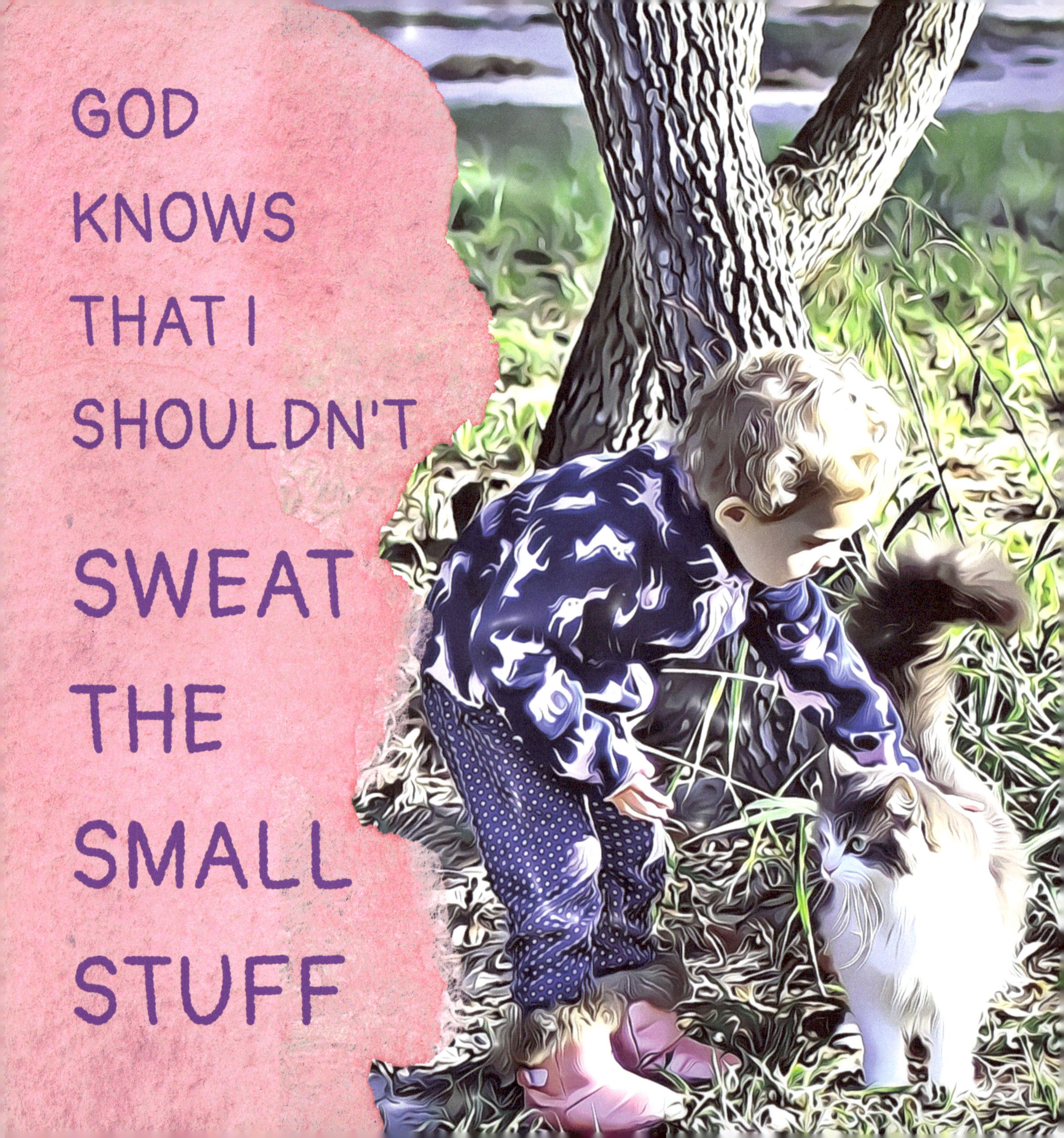

GOD
KNOWS
THAT I
SHOULDN'T
SWEAT
THE
SMALL
STUFF

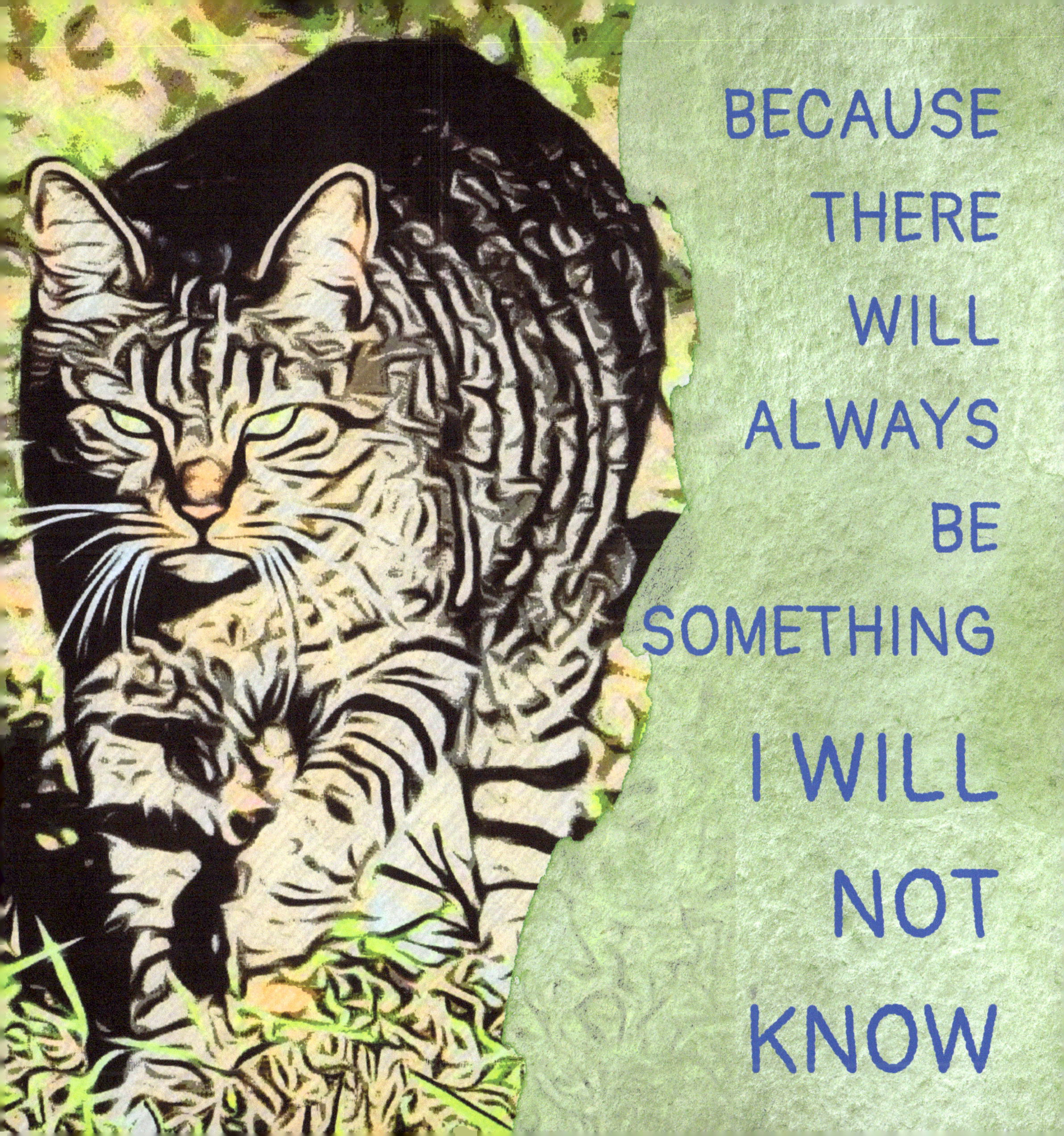
BECAUSE
THERE
WILL
ALWAYS
BE
SOMETHING
I WILL
NOT
KNOW

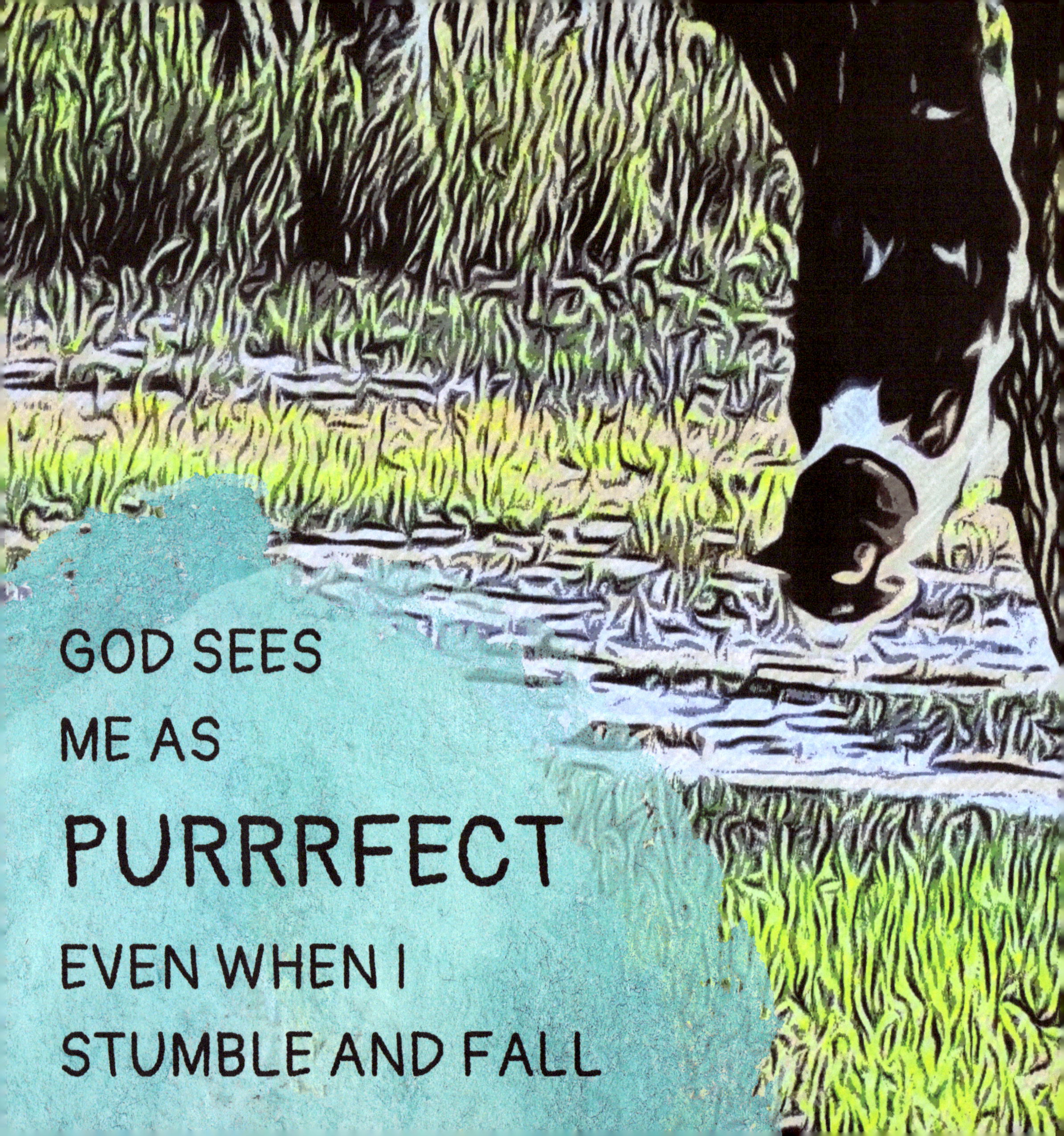

GOD SEES
ME AS
PURRRFECT
EVEN WHEN I
STUMBLE AND FALL

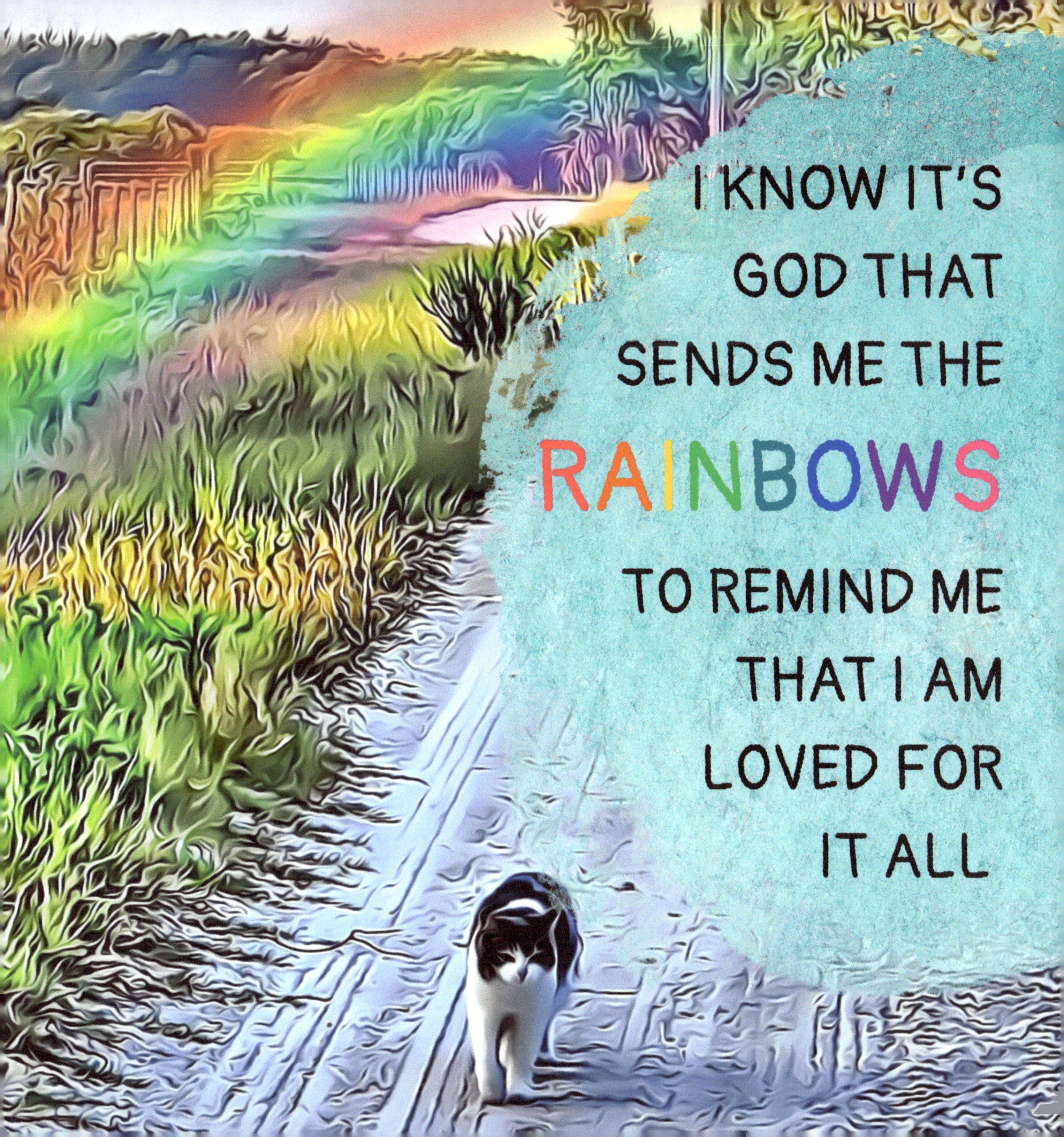

I KNOW IT'S GOD THAT SENDS ME THE RAINBOWS TO REMIND ME THAT I AM LOVED FOR IT ALL

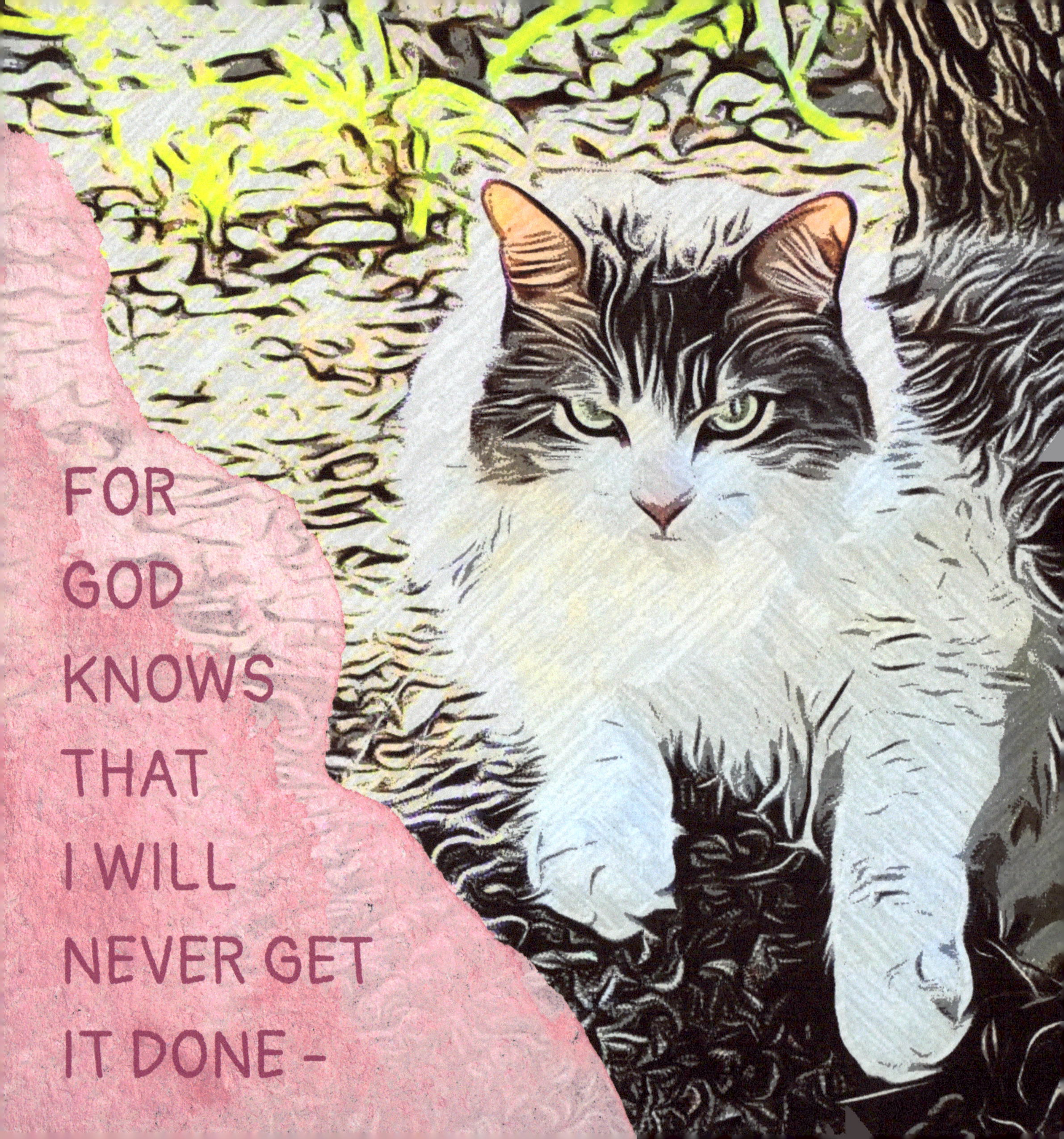

FOR
GOD
KNOWS
THAT
I WILL
NEVER GET
IT DONE -

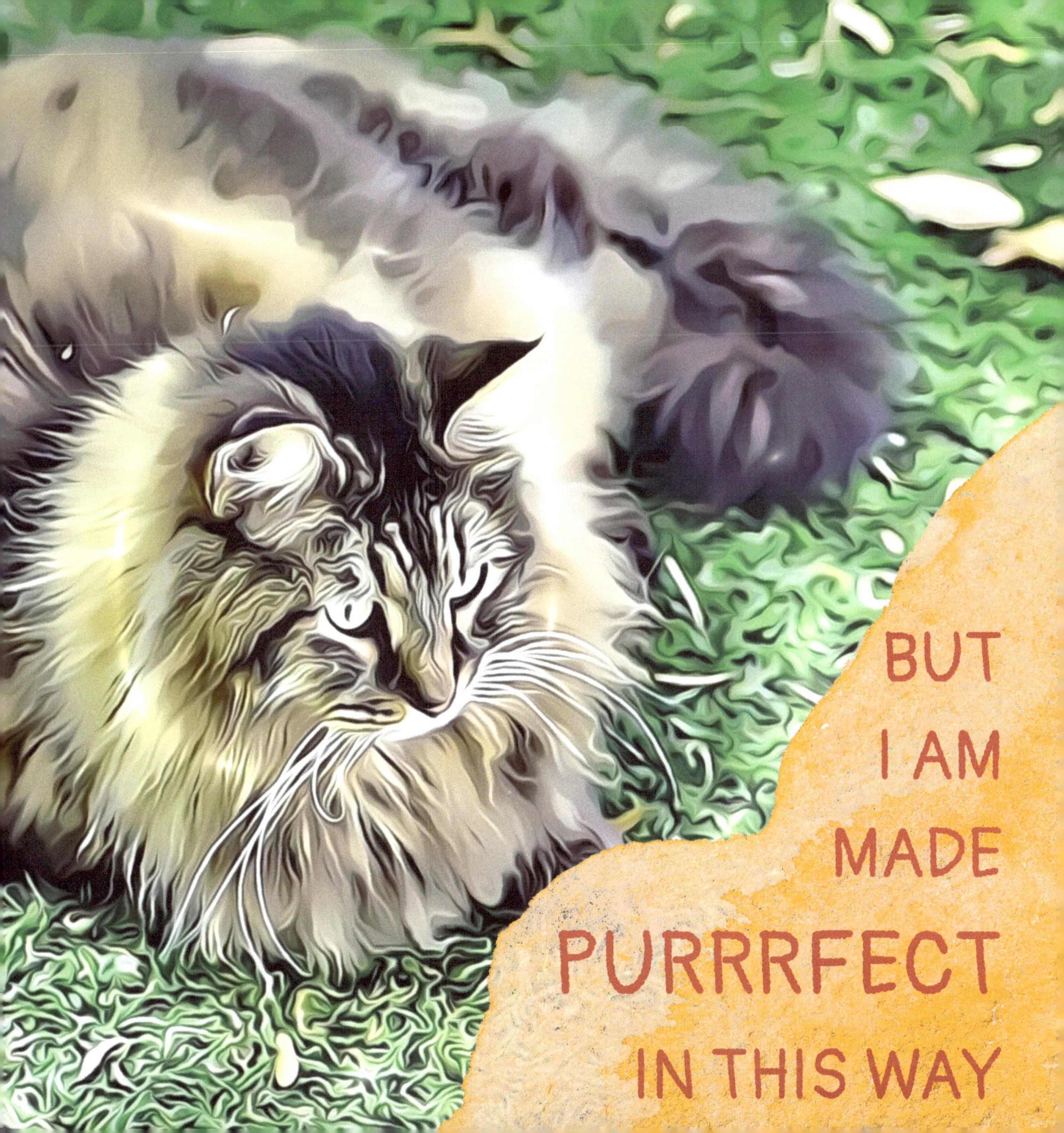
BUT
I AM
MADE
PURRRFECT
IN THIS WAY

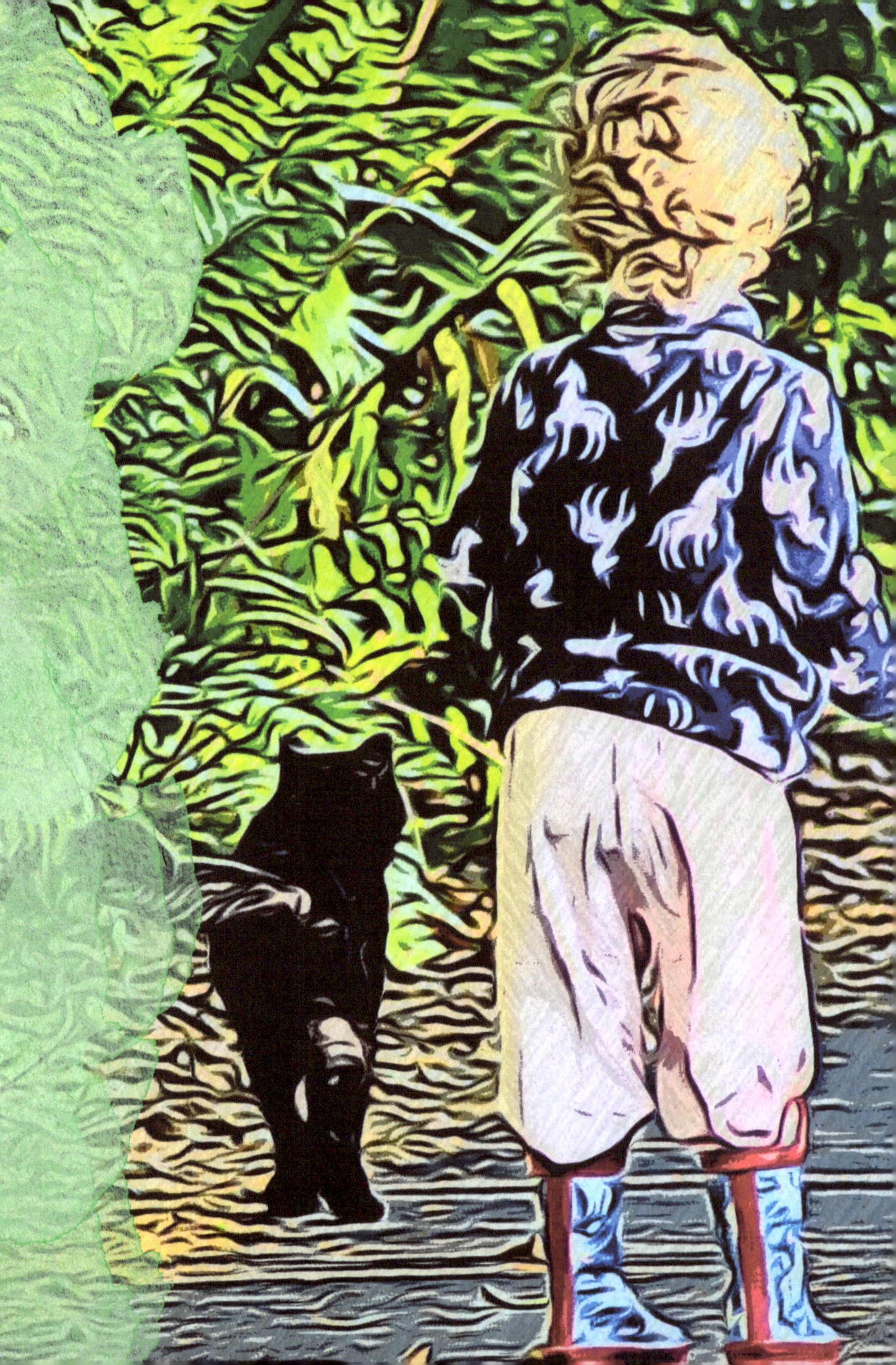

I AM A
NEVER
ENDING
WORK
OF
ART –

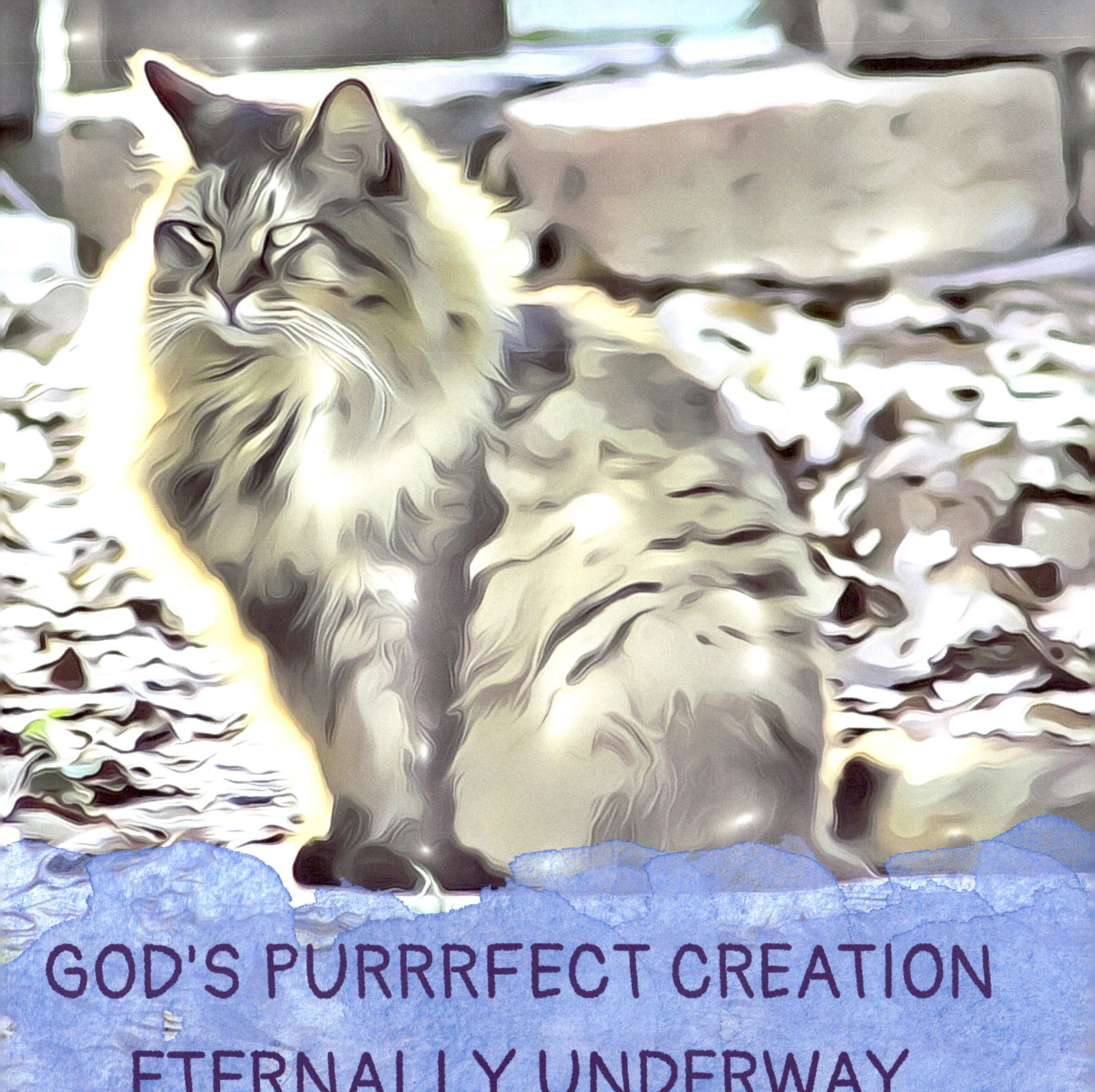
GOD'S PURRRFECT CREATION
ETERNALLY UNDERWAY

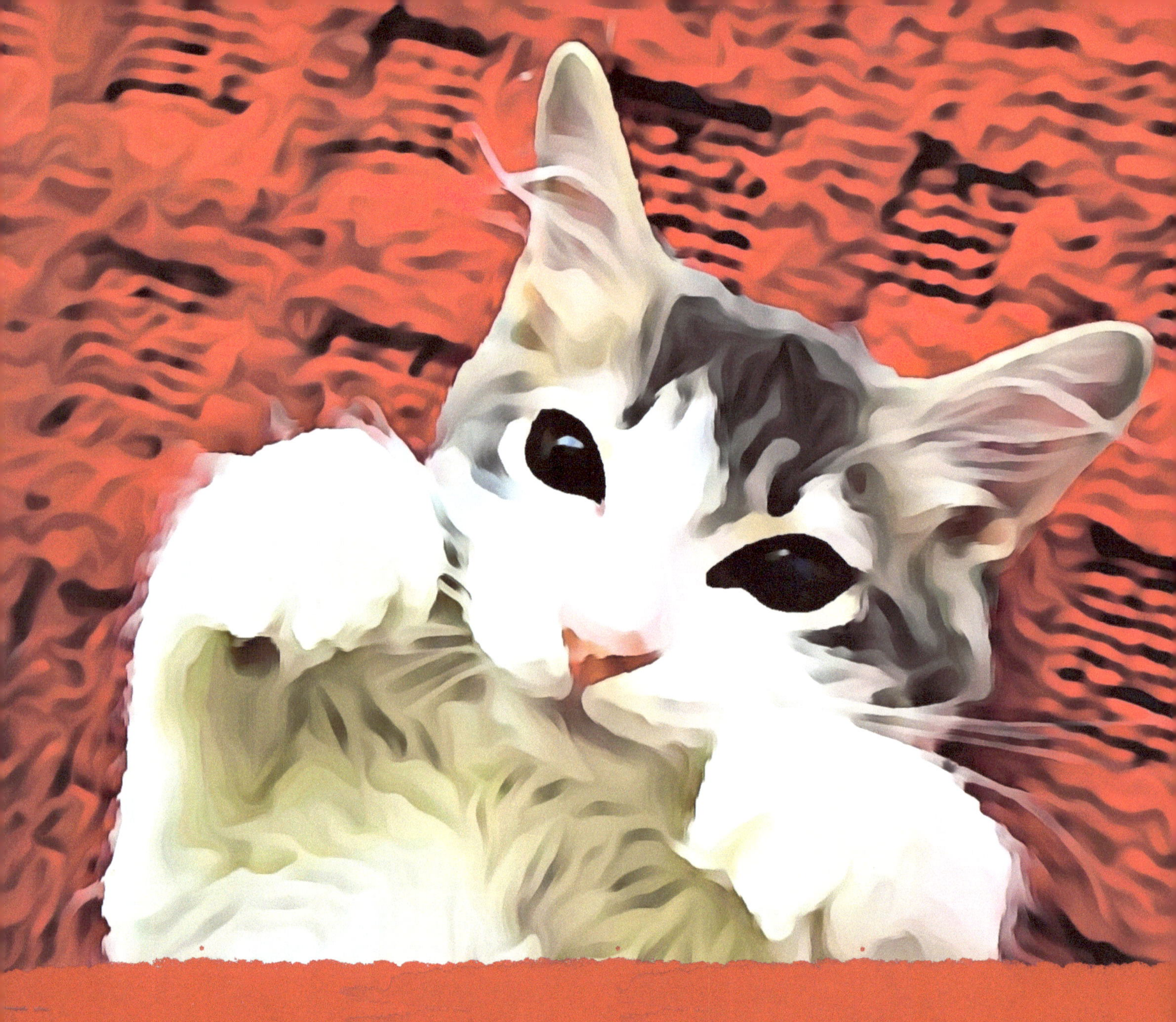
AND IN THE END I WILL NEVER
STOP SHOWING UP TO BE...

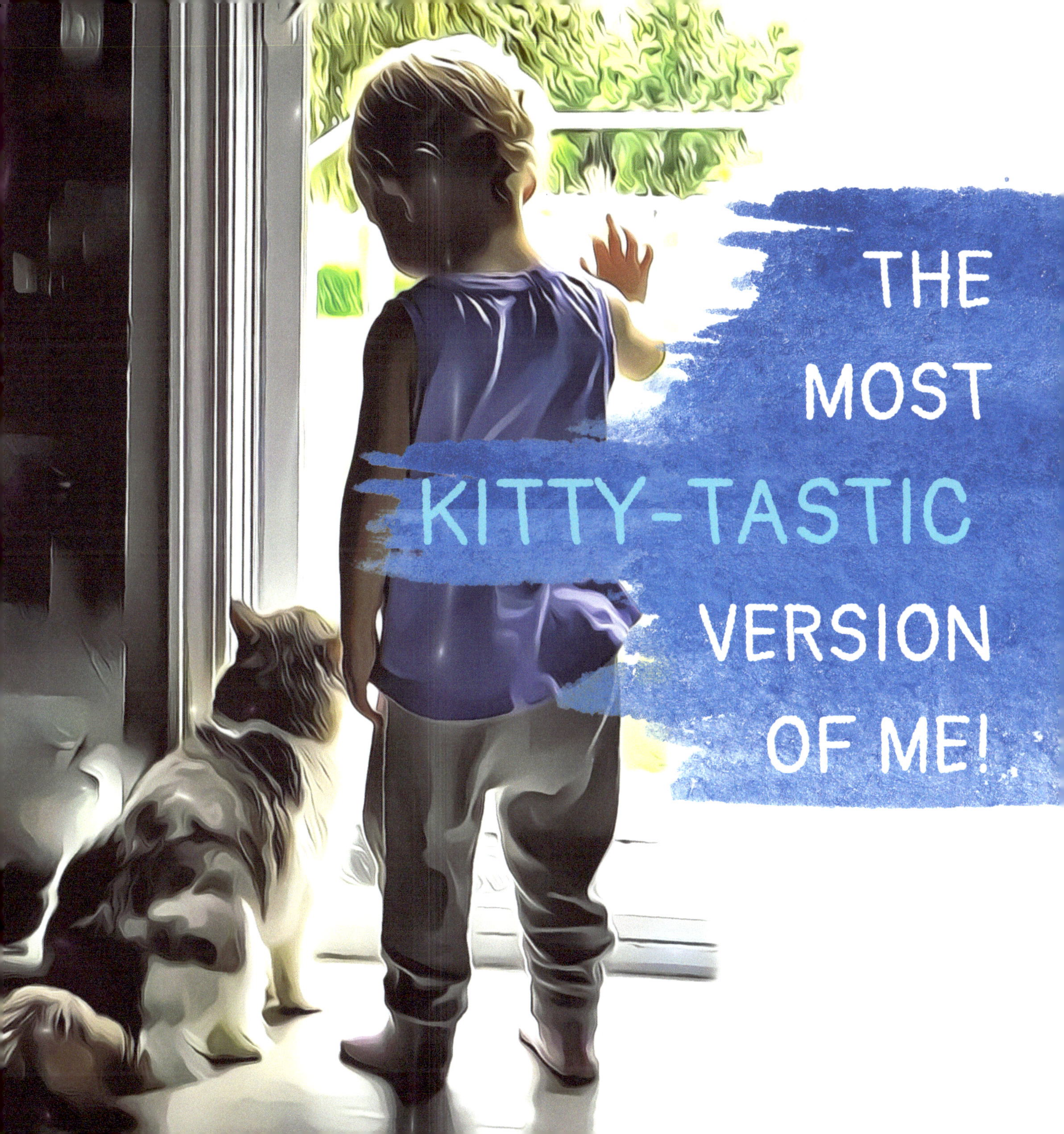

THE
MOST
KITTY-TASTIC
VERSION
OF ME!

www.ingramcontent.com/pod-product-compliance
Lightning Source LLC
Chambersburg PA
CBHW042134030726
47599CB00002B/474